PODCASTARS

ADRIANA LUNA CARLOS

Editor-In-Chief, Designer
and Co-Founder

HANNA OLIVAS

Managing Editor &
Co-Founder

NICOLE CURTIS

Director of the SRS
Magazine Division

ADVERTISING OPPORTUNITIES

Info@SheRisesStudios.com

PODCASTARS MAGAZINE
MAY 2025

SHE RISES
STUDIOS

CONTACT US

SheRisesStudios@gmail.com

WWW.SHERISESSTUDIOS.COM

LETTER FROM THE EDITORS

Dear Reader,

Podcasting is more than a trend—it's a lifeline, a catalyst for healing, and a revolution in storytelling. At its essence, podcasting is about truth-telling in real time. It's where we meet our raw edges, process our pain, and share our resilience so that others know they're not alone. This special issue, Voices of Resilience: Celebrating Podcasting During Mental Health Awareness Month, honors those creators who are courageously shaping conversations around emotional wellness, identity, and transformation through the power of their voice.

On our cover is the unapologetic and trailblazing Yuliana Hartanto, a force who is redefining what leadership, femininity, and success sound like. With her bold podcast, she dismantles the hustle narrative and invites women to reclaim their soft power, their truth, and their space. Yuliana is not just sharing wisdom—she's initiating a return to wholeness.

Throughout these pages, you'll discover podcast hosts who are rewriting the script—turning their own healing journeys into powerful platforms for change. Whether they're sharing vulnerable stories or offering guidance through lived experience, their voices echo with strength, purpose, and impact.

We hope this edition reminds you that your voice matters. Every story shared is a bridge built. Every truth spoken is a spark ignited. And together, through sound and story, we rise.

Warm regards,

Adriana Luna Carlos, Hanna Olivas and Nicole Curtis
Editors of PODCASTARS Magazine

SHE WINS

GLOBAL SUMMIT 2025

This is more than an event—it's a movement!

Join 500+ unstoppable women for two days of powerful keynotes, celebrity fireside chats, business growth strategies, and high-level networking. Elevate your career, expand your influence, and connect with industry leaders shaping the future!

Want To Take The Stage!

We're inviting dynamic speakers to share expertise on finance, leadership, branding, health, tech, and more! Elevate your voice, gain global exposure on FENIX TV, and unlock Exclusive Speaker Perks worth over $2,000!

Apply to Speak Today!

 https://form.jotform.com/250646617740156

NOVEMBER 6-7 2025 | **LAS VEGAS, NEVADA**

FROM HUSTLE TO HARMONY:

How **Yuliana Hartanto** is Redefining Leadership Through Worth, Wisdom, and Wealth

In a world that often equates success with sacrifice and ambition with burnout, Yuliana Hartanto is leading a revolution—one podcast episode at a time. As the founder and voice behind The Affluent CEO Podcast, Yuliana is reshaping the narrative for high-achieving women by offering a new paradigm: one rooted in worth, not hustle.

With a background in managing billion-dollar corporate contracts and scaling an e-commerce business to $20K weeks, Yuliana is not new to strategy or success. But her journey from boardroom burnout to embodied leadership wasn't paved with spreadsheets or sales funnels. It was marked by something far more powerful—coming home to her truth.

"The Affluent CEO was born from a deep knowing that the old paradigm of success—built on burnout, people-pleasing, and proving—is not sustainable for visionary women," she shares. *"This podcast is my love letter to the woman who is ready to stop negotiating against herself and start leading from her innate power, intuition, and divine alignment."*

Strategy Meets Soul
Yuliana's unique brilliance lies in her ability to blend the strategic mind of a CPA-qualified negotiator with the intuitive wisdom of an energy healer. Every episode of The Affluent CEO Podcast isn't just about business growth—it's an invitation to rise into feminine power without abandoning logic.

"Strategy without soul is like driving with two people arguing over directions," she says. *"You're moving, but not aligned."* Her episodes often merge frameworks on negotiation or wealth-building with deep somatic practices and energetic recalibrations.

At the core of her work is the question: What does my listener need to hear to remember who she truly is? For Yuliana, this isn't about offering advice—it's about activating remembrance.

The Power of Effortless Asking
One of her signature teachings is the concept of *"effortless asking"*—the radical idea that women are allowed to want more, not because they've earned it, but because they exist.

The results speak volumes. One listener asked for a $50K raise after years of silence—and received it. Another left a toxic business partnership and tripled her income. But beyond the numbers are even more powerful breakthroughs: internal revolutions where women stop apologizing for their desires and start owning their voice.

"It's not just about language," she explains. *"It's about redefining and embodying your next-level identity."*

Rewriting the Subconscious
Yuliana doesn't shy away from tackling imposter syndrome and generational programming. Her episodes explore how trauma is stored in the body, how beliefs are passed down, and how reclaiming one's nervous system is the key to reclaiming one's life.

"Imposter syndrome is often a symptom of deeper self-abandonment," she says. *"My podcast isn't here to fix you—it's here to free you."*

This freedom comes through somatic awareness, identity reinvention, and energetic expansion. Through storytelling and spiritual intelligence, she helps her listeners rewrite the script they've unconsciously inherited.

A Sacred Shift
Yuliana's own sacred shift happened during a life-changing retreat called *Quantum Being.* It was there, guided by her mentor, that she wrote out her life story and was met with a vision of her younger self—craving love, earning validation through perfectionism, and playing the *"good girl."*

Photography by Erika Bencs Photography, www.instagram.com/erikabencsphotography

"That moment cracked something open in me," she recalls. *"I realized I'd built my identity around being chosen, being seen, being perfect. And I was exhausted."*

It was this breakthrough that catalyzed her transformation into the woman she is today: deeply intuitive, wildly successful, and unapologetically aligned.

"Now, I no longer chase success. I magnetize it by becoming the woman who is already living her new reality."

Embodied Leadership

These days, success for Yuliana isn't measured in revenue—it's felt in alignment. Her daily rituals reflect this shift: breathwork, future self-visualizations, dancing, and tuning into the wisdom of her body.

"True power is cyclical, not linear," she says. *"Stillness is a business strategy."*

She listens to her body like it's a business partner, honoring its cues and aligning her decisions with her internal rhythm. This feminine-led approach is a stark contrast to the grind culture that so often dominates entrepreneurship—and it's what makes The Affluent CEO so magnetic.

The Future is Feminine—and Free

Looking ahead, Yuliana is expanding her podcast into an immersive platform for transformation. Future episodes will feature women from every walk of life—from corporate boardrooms to sacred jungles—exploring themes like erotic leadership, nervous system-led strategy, wealth consciousness, and embodied power.

She's also planning live podcast experiences that bring listeners into the room for real-time breakthroughs.

"We're not just talking about leadership," she says. *"We're experiencing it, embodying it, and rewriting what it means to be a wealthy, powerful, purpose-led woman."*

Wealth as a Catalyst for Global Change

But Yuliana's mission reaches beyond personal development—it's rooted in systemic transformation. As a fierce advocate for ending gender-based violence and poverty, she views wealth as more than currency. To her, it's a tool for liberation.

"When a woman reclaims her voice, she stops accepting less. When she knows her worth, she stops settling. When she builds wealth, she transforms generations," Yuliana explains.

Her work is not just about helping individual women rise—it's about dismantling outdated systems and co-creating a world where empowered women empower others.

Becoming Unbecoming

Her bestselling book, *Unbecoming You: 21 Days to Live Life on Your Own Terms*, is a raw, soul-baring guide to shedding the identities we were taught to wear and stepping into our divine truth.

"The belief I had to unbecome was that love had to be earned through performance," she reflects. *"I spent years proving my worth—until I realized I was already chosen. By life. By purpose. By the divine."*

That, she says, is the heart of unbecoming: it's not about losing yourself—it's about remembering yourself.

Yuliana Hartanto isn't just hosting a podcast—she's dismantling the hustle paradigm and calling women back to their unapologetic, untamed power. Through her words, her wisdom, and her unwavering belief in feminine power, she is guiding a generation of women to stop performing, start receiving, and finally take their place as affluent CEOs—not just of companies, but of their lives.

Because the truth is: success isn't about doing more. It's about being more of who you already are.

Photography by Erika Bencs Photography,
www.instagram.com/erikabencsphotography

Connect With Yuliana

www.instagram.com/yuliana_francie
www.facebook.com/YulianaFrancie
www.linkedin.com/in/yulianafrancie
www.yulianafrancie.com
www.youtube.com/@Yuliana_Francie
https://open.spotify.com/show/2dhken7J25qyjV3t2CEyaS?si=480a33fb8f40463d
https://podcasts.apple.com/us/podcast/the-affluent-ceo-show-the-select-circles-codes-to/id1800138616

DR. ALEXANDRA SOLOMON:

The Voice of Love, Happiness, and Healing

In the evolving landscape of mental health awareness, few voices have resonated as deeply and consistently as that of Dr. Alexandra Solomon. A renowned clinical psychologist, professor, and bestselling author, Dr. Solomon has carved a unique space at the intersection of emotional wellness, intimate relationships, and self-compassion. Through her widely acclaimed The Love, Happiness, and Success Podcast, she continues to be a guiding light for listeners navigating the complexity of human connection and inner healing.

At a time when mental health is more openly discussed than ever —yet still misunderstood in many ways—Dr. Solomon is part of a vital cultural shift. She isn't just talking about therapy. She's translating the language of psychology into stories, insights, and tangible tools that people can use in their everyday lives. And in doing so, she is modeling something both courageous and deeply needed: the kind of radical emotional honesty that creates lasting change.

Dr. Solomon brings to her podcast what she brings to every client session and classroom: a deep respect for the human experience. Trained as a relational therapist and seasoned in academia, she has the rare ability to pair scientific rigor with heartfelt vulnerability. Her podcast isn't about speaking at her audience—it's a conversation with them.

Every episode of The Love, Happiness, and Success Podcast explores a facet of emotional wellness—whether it's healing after heartbreak, navigating the dynamics of a long-term relationship, or building a healthier sense of self. What makes Dr. Solomon's approach remarkable is how she validates the listener's experience while gently challenging them to grow. She champions self-care not as an indulgence, but as a necessity. She frames emotional resilience not as an inherited trait, but as a skill that anyone can learn—with the right guidance and support.

One of the most powerful aspects of Dr. Solomon's work is her emphasis on how our relationships mirror our inner world. For her, love is not just a romantic endeavor—it's a practice ground for healing, boundaries, and transformation. She often reminds listeners that the health of our relationships directly impacts our mental health, and vice versa.

In today's digital age, where disconnection can be masked by likes and scrolls, Dr. Solomon's message feels revolutionary. She invites her audience to drop into deeper awareness—not just of how they feel, but of what those feelings are asking for. Her teachings are grounded in the idea that love begins within. We cannot show up for others until we learn how to show up for ourselves. And healing doesn't always look like dramatic breakthroughs; sometimes, it's simply the act of pausing to ask, *"What do I need right now?"*

What sets Dr. Solomon apart in the podcasting world is her unwavering commitment to authenticity. She doesn't sugarcoat the challenges of being human. She doesn't offer quick fixes or one-size-fits-all advice. Instead, she holds space for complexity. In her episodes, it's okay to be both hurting and hopeful. It's okay to love someone and still need boundaries. It's okay to want happiness while grieving something you've lost.

This honesty is what builds trust. And it's what makes her podcast a refuge for so many. Listeners often describe feeling seen, heard, and empowered after tuning in. They walk away not just with insights, but with a renewed sense of possibility. That is the essence of resilience—not the absence of struggle, but the ability to meet it with grace, courage, and support.

During Mental Health Awareness Month, it's voices like Dr. Alexandra Solomon's that remind us why podcasting is more than a platform—it's a movement. It's a way to reach people where they are, in their cars, at the gym, while folding laundry or walking through heartbreak. Podcasts like hers democratize access to mental health wisdom, creating ripple effects of healing across the world.

As we celebrate the voices of resilience this month, Dr. Solomon stands as a beacon—illuminating the path to emotional wellness with every word, every episode, and every courageous question she invites us to ask ourselves.

Her work is not just a gift to the mental health field. It's a gift to humanity.

www.sherisesstudios.com

Is Manifesting
Bullshit?
Podcast
Host: Cindy Witteman

Is Manifesting
Bullshit?
Podcast

By Cindy Witteman

IS *MANIFESTING* BULLSHIT?

Podcast Unfiltered Conversations on Life, Dreams, and Manifesting

The world of manifesting is filled with passion, controversy, and extraordinary personal journeys. The *"Is Manifesting Bullshit? Podcast"* dives into these discussions, bringing together skeptics, critics, and believers from around the world to share their real life experiences. Each week the podcast offers inspiring conversations that explore how manifesting has shaped the lives of its guests. Some have achieved the life of their dreams through manifestation, some remain unsure if it is fact or fiction, and others have stories that fall somewhere in between.

Before the podcast even began the original Is Manifesting Bullshit? book was published. This groundbreaking book challenged conventional wisdom about manifesting and went on to win the International Impact Book Award in 2023. Its blend of personal stories and practical insights set the stage for a broader conversation that would later be carried forward by the podcast.

Once the book made an impact, the podcast emerged as a natural extension of its themes. Each episode features interviews with guests who share unique manifesting journeys. Some reveal how they manifested the life of their dreams, recounting the moments when their aspirations became reality. Others question whether manifesting is a true force or simply a placebo effect. The authentic and unfiltered approach of the podcast creates a space where all viewpoints are welcomed, challenging and inspiring listeners to examine their own beliefs about manifestation.

Following the podcasts success the conversation evolved further with the release of Is Manifesting Bullshit? Part 2 The Limit Is You. This second book, coming after the podcast was established, gathers authors from around the world who share their personal manifesting stories. The contributors explore the idea that the only true limit is the one we impose on ourselves, offering a global perspective on the power of manifestation. Both books have become international best sellers and are celebrated for their raw honesty and transformative insights.

For those eager to dive deeper into the world of manifesting, autographed copies of both books are available on our website at cfviews.com. Whether you are a staunch believer, a curious skeptic, or simply someone who enjoys a good story of personal triumph, these books provide valuable perspectives on the complexities of manifesting.

The Is Manifesting Bullshit? Podcast and its accompanying books have sparked a global conversation about the power of manifestation. From the original book that paved the way to the podcast that expanded the dialogue, and finally to Part 2 that brings together voices from across the globe, this project has evolved into a dynamic exploration of what it means to manifest change in our lives. Each episode and every page reminds us that the line between success and skepticism is often blurred but within that space lies the possibility for extraordinary transformation.

Tune in to the podcast, pick up a copy of our international best selling books, and join the conversation as we continue to explore the limitless potential of manifesting.

Connect With Cindy

www.cfviews.com/is-manifesting-bullshit
www.facebook.com/profile.php?id=61550654840372

FENIX TV

YOUR PLATFORM, YOUR VOICE, YOUR POWER!

Step into the Spotlight as a Host on FENIX TV!

Are you ready to amplify your message, inspire others, and be part of a groundbreaking network dedicated to **empowering women worldwide**? FENIX TV is your platform to **shine as a host**, share your expertise, and connect with a global audience.

WHY HOST ON FENIX TV?

- Reach a worldwide audience passionate about empowerment
- Showcase your voice, brand, and expertise
- Join a community of inspiring leaders and changemakers
- Be part of a network that uplifts and celebrates women

Whether you dream of leading a talk show, sharing powerful stories, or educating and inspiring others—FENIX TV is where your voice matters!

SPOTS ARE LIMITED! Secure your hosting opportunity today.

 Contact us now at
info@fenixtv.app

 Learn more at
https://fenixtv.app

KEVIN HINES:
A Voice of Survival, Purpose, and Hope

There are some stories that don't just inspire—they transform. Kevin Hines's story is one of those. As a suicide attempt survivor, award-winning filmmaker, mental health advocate, and host of The HINDSIGHT Podcast, Kevin has turned his personal pain into a global mission of healing and hope. His voice is not only powerful—it's life-saving.

In 2000, at the age of 19, Kevin jumped off the Golden Gate Bridge in an attempt to take his own life. Miraculously, he survived. What could have been the end of his story instead became the beginning of a profound calling. In the decades since, Kevin has devoted his life to speaking out about mental health, suicide prevention, and the resilience of the human spirit. His podcast, The HINDSIGHT Podcast, is an extension of that mission —an unflinching, compassionate, and deeply human exploration of what it means to survive, thrive, and serve others through lived experience.

Unlike many wellness platforms that gently circle around the subject of suicide, Kevin walks straight into it—not with fear, but with reverence and truth. He speaks from the inside out, using his own journey to break through stigma and ignite life-affirming conversations. His openness disarms. His honesty dissects shame. His vulnerability empowers listeners to speak, feel, and fight for their lives.

Each episode of The HINDSIGHT Podcast is an invitation: to listen, to learn, and to live. Kevin interviews fellow survivors, clinicians, advocates, and public figures, all of whom share a deep commitment to mental health awareness and suicide prevention. These aren't just stories of survival—they're testimonies of transformation. Kevin weaves his own reflections into each episode, grounding every conversation in truth, empathy, and purpose.

What sets Kevin apart is his relentless belief in the value of every human life—including those in the deepest trenches of despair. He knows what it's like to feel hopeless. He knows the power of one kind word, one helping hand, one voice that says, *"You matter."* Through his podcast, he becomes that voice for thousands of listeners across the globe.

Kevin's work goes beyond awareness—it's about action. He advocates for better mental health resources, crisis support systems, and education. He challenges harmful narratives and calls out the silence that so often surrounds suicide. And he does it all while reminding people that it's okay to struggle, that healing is possible, and that asking for help is a sign of strength, not weakness.

Mental Health Awareness Month is not only about education— it's about amplifying the voices that give others the courage to keep going. Kevin Hines is one of those voices. His story is not sugar-coated, and that's exactly why it resonates. He tells the hard truths. He shares the difficult moments. But through it all, his message never wavers: Stay. Your life has purpose. You are not alone.

Kevin's message also reaches beyond individuals—it touches families, friends, communities, and systems. He educates people on the warning signs of mental health crises, the importance of checking in, and the ripple effect of compassion. His words are a reminder that everyone has a role to play in suicide prevention. We can all be a lifeline for someone.

In a world where so many are silently hurting, The HINDSIGHT Podcast serves as both a mirror and a light. It reflects the raw reality of mental illness while offering a path forward—a path paved with resilience, connection, and truth. Kevin never promises an easy journey, but he does offer something even more powerful: solidarity. The knowledge that others have walked this road and found their way through.

As we honor the voices of resilience this month, Kevin Hines stands as a beacon. He is proof that even in our darkest hour, there can be a second chance. That our scars do not define us— they shape us. That our survival is not an accident—it's a calling. Kevin Hines did not just survive. He chose to live. And through every episode, every speech, and every story he shares, he's helping others choose life, too.

SHE RISES
STUDIOS

JOIN THE SRS COMMUNITY

WHERE WOMEN RISE TOGETHER!

Connect. Empower. Thrive. Whether you're an entrepreneur, professional, or simply seeking inspiration, **this is your space to grow!**

- Daily Motivation
- Expert Insights
- Sisterhood & Support

You don't have to do it alone—let's rise together!

JOIN NOW!

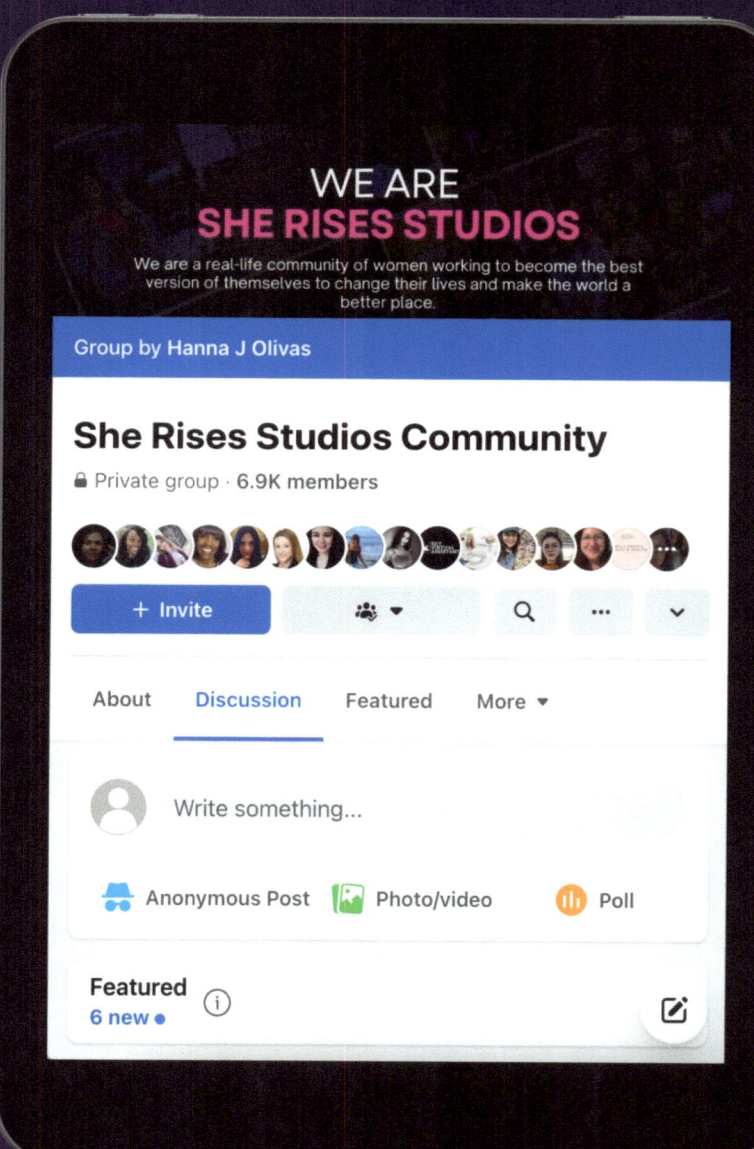

GET YOUR COPY NOW

Celebrate the power of women through inspiring stories and insights.

From Surviving to Thriving
Gina Stockdall

Shifting Narratives
Anita Comisky and Michelle Belloit

Stepping into Wadzi:
Lessons from my life
Wadzanai Garwe

Garden to Kitchen Planner
Ines Batterton

Invisible to Visible
Julie Lavia

Unlearn the Crap and Level Up
Kathy Baldwin

DR. JOY HARDEN BRADFORD:

Changing the Conversation Through "Therapy for Black Girls"

In the ever-expanding world of podcasting, few voices have made as profound and necessary an impact as Dr. Joy Harden Bradford. A licensed psychologist, speaker, and mental health advocate, Dr. Joy is the creator and host of the widely acclaimed Therapy for Black Girls podcast—an empowering and deeply resonant space where mental health, self-care, and personal growth are centered through a culturally competent lens. Her work has not only broken barriers in the mental health field but has also given voice to countless women who have long been underserved and underrepresented in these conversations.

As we celebrate Mental Health Awareness Month under the theme Voices of Resilience, Dr. Joy's podcast stands as a shining example of what it means to blend vulnerability with expertise, compassion with clarity, and personal storytelling with professional insight. With over 300 episodes and a global audience, Therapy for Black Girls is more than a podcast—it's a movement.

When Dr. Joy launched the podcast in 2017, her goal was simple but powerful: to create a safe space where Black women could explore mental health topics that resonated with their real-life experiences. She recognized a glaring gap in the mental health world—while conversations around therapy were becoming more mainstream, they often failed to speak directly to the unique emotional, cultural, and systemic challenges faced by Black women.

From the beginning, Therapy for Black Girls has tackled subjects like anxiety, trauma, boundary setting, relationships, burnout, and imposter syndrome with warmth and relatability. Dr. Joy's voice—equal parts soothing and empowering—offers listeners not only insight but validation. Whether she's joined by a guest expert or speaking solo, every episode is rooted in the belief that Black women deserve access to culturally responsive mental health care and the tools to thrive emotionally.

What sets Dr. Joy apart isn't just her clinical expertise—it's her unwavering commitment to humanizing the therapy process. She helps dismantle long-standing stigmas around seeking help by normalizing therapy as an act of strength, not weakness.

She reminds her audience that therapy is not only for when life feels unbearable; it's also for maintenance, growth, and joy. Through engaging conversations and actionable advice, she makes mental wellness feel accessible, relevant, and even joyful.

Dr. Joy's influence goes beyond the podcast mic. She created a national therapist directory specifically for Black women seeking culturally competent care, a resource that has helped thousands of women connect with mental health professionals who truly understand their lived experiences. This initiative alone has been a game-changer in making therapy feel less intimidating and more affirming.

The Therapy for Black Girls community has grown into a powerful digital sisterhood. From social media to live events, listeners regularly share how the podcast has encouraged them to start therapy, set healthy boundaries, or simply feel seen in a world that too often overlooks them. It's not uncommon to hear stories of women who, after years of struggling in silence, finally found the language and support they needed to heal—all because they pressed play on an episode.

In this season of reflection and mental health awareness, Dr. Joy's work reminds us of a crucial truth: representation in mental health spaces matters. When people hear voices that reflect their own, when their pain is understood without explanation, and when healing is framed as both possible and deserved—they are more likely to begin their journey toward well-being.

Resilience is not just about bouncing back. It's about feeling deeply, growing intentionally, and making space for rest, joy, and connection. Dr. Joy Harden Bradford has helped thousands embrace that kind of resilience, one meaningful conversation at a time. Her podcast continues to be a beacon of light for those seeking clarity, care, and community.

As Mental Health Awareness Month continues, let us honor and uplift the voices that challenge stigma and champion healing. Let us amplify the work of leaders like Dr. Joy who remind us that mental health is a fundamental part of our overall well-being. And let us continue building a world where seeking therapy is celebrated, not whispered about—where every voice, especially those historically unheard, is empowered to speak, heal, and rise.

THE WHISPERS OF WELLNESS:

How Mental Health Podcasts Illuminated My Path from Postpartum Darkness to Entrepreneurial Light

By Grace Olayiwola

The journey into motherhood is often painted in hues of radiant joy and unconditional love. While those colors certainly exist, my own introduction to this transformative experience was also deeply shadowed by the insidious grip of postpartum depression (PPD). The vibrant world around me felt muted, joy became a foreign concept, and the simplest tasks loomed like insurmountable mountains. It was a period of profound isolation, where the very essence of my being felt fractured.

In the suffocating silence of my struggle, a faint whisper began to penetrate the darkness: mental health podcasts. Initially, they were a hesitant exploration, a stolen moment during a restless night or a quiet afternoon. But gradually, these voices became lifelines, offering solace, validation, and a profound sense of not being alone. As the founder of ALG Studio Store, a brand dedicated to curated wellness and self-care gifts, and ALG Elysian Flames Co., a purveyor of handcrafted wellness candles, my personal journey through PPD and the transformative power of mental health podcasts have become inextricably linked to the very ethos of my businesses. These platforms didn't just offer information; they ignited a spark of courage within me, a desire to break the silence and, ultimately, inspired the very foundations of my brands, rooted in the belief that nurturing mental well-being is paramount.

Mental health-focused podcasts are not merely audio files; they are digital sanctuaries, offering a diverse tapestry of perspectives, expert insights, and lived experiences. They are democratizing access to mental health information, breaking down stigma, and fostering a sense of community for listeners who might otherwise feel isolated in their struggles. The beauty of this medium lies in its accessibility. Whether you're folding laundry, commuting to work, or simply seeking a moment of quiet reflection, these podcasts are readily available, offering a confidential and non-judgmental space to explore complex emotions and learn practical coping mechanisms.

For me, during the throes of PPD, the voices of therapists, survivors, and advocates became beacons of hope. Hearing others articulate the very feelings that felt so alien and terrifying within me was profoundly validating. It chipped away at the shame and the feeling that I was somehow failing as a mother.

Podcasts like *"The Hilarious World of Depression,"* which blends humor with honest conversations about mental illness, helped me find moments of levity amidst the darkness. Others, featuring clinical psychologists and psychiatrists, provided valuable insights into the neurobiology of depression and offered evidence-based strategies for managing symptoms.

The impact of these podcasts extended beyond mere information. They fostered a sense of connection. Hearing individuals share their vulnerabilities, their triumphs, and their ongoing journeys created a powerful sense of solidarity. It was a reminder that mental health challenges are a shared human experience, not a personal failing. This sense of community was instrumental in dismantling the wall of isolation that PPD had erected around me.

Furthermore, mental health podcasts empowered me to advocate for my own well-being. Learning about different therapeutic modalities, self-care practices, and the importance of seeking professional help gave me the courage to reach out. It armed me with the language to articulate my struggles and the knowledge to navigate the often-daunting landscape of mental healthcare.

This personal transformation is deeply woven into the fabric of ALG Studio Store and ALG Elysian Flames Co. My experience with PPD underscored the critical need for accessible and compassionate self-care resources. ALG Studio Store was born from the desire to curate a collection of items that encourage mindful moments and nurture inner peace. From soothing aromatherapy candles to journals designed for self-reflection, each product is thoughtfully chosen to support holistic well-being.

Similarly, ALG Elysian Flames Co. emerged from the understanding that sensory experiences can profoundly impact our emotional state. The gentle flicker of a candle, infused with calming essential oils, can create a sanctuary of tranquility amidst the chaos of daily life. Each scent is carefully selected to evoke feelings of peace, grounding, and comfort, serving as a gentle reminder to prioritize self-nurturing.

The influence of mental health podcasts is palpable in the very essence of my brands. The emphasis on open conversations about mental well-being, the focus on accessible self-care practices, and the creation of products that foster emotional comfort are all direct reflections of the transformative impact these audio resources had on my own journey.

The rise of mental health-focused podcasts signifies a significant shift in how we approach mental well-being. They are transforming listener experiences by:

Reducing Stigma: By openly discussing mental health challenges, these podcasts normalize conversations that were once shrouded in shame and silence. Hearing relatable stories from diverse individuals helps listeners feel less alone and more willing to seek help.

Increasing Awareness and Education: They provide accessible and digestible information about various mental health conditions, treatment options, and coping strategies, empowering listeners to understand their own experiences and advocate for their needs.

Fostering a Sense of Community: The parasocial relationships formed with hosts and the shared experiences discussed create a sense of belonging and validation for listeners who may feel isolated in their struggles.

Offering Practical Tools and Techniques: Many podcasts feature experts who share actionable advice and practical tools for managing stress, anxiety, depression, and other mental health concerns.

Inspiring Hope and Resilience: Hearing stories of recovery and resilience offers hope to those who are struggling and reinforces the message that healing is possible.

Democratizing Access to Information: Podcasts are often free and readily available, making mental health information accessible to a wider audience, regardless of geographical location or socioeconomic status.

My journey from the depths of postpartum depression to becoming a founder of wellness-focused brands is a testament to the power of connection, information, and the courage to speak openly about mental health. Mental health podcasts were instrumental in this transformation, offering me a lifeline during a dark period and inspiring the very core values of ALG Studio Store and ALG Elysian Flames Co.

These audio sanctuaries are more than just entertainment; they are catalysts for change, transforming listener experiences by fostering understanding, reducing stigma, and empowering individuals to prioritize their mental well-being. As I continue to navigate the complexities of motherhood and entrepreneurship, the lessons learned from those early days of listening remain a guiding force, reminding me of the profound impact that open conversations and accessible resources can have on the lives of individuals seeking solace and healing. And it is with this understanding that I strive to create products and a brand ethos that echoes the very whispers of wellness that once guided me towards the light.

Connect With Grace

Instagram: @AlgstudioStore_LLC
www.algstudiostore.com
Instagram: @ALGelysianflames
www.algelysianflamesco.com

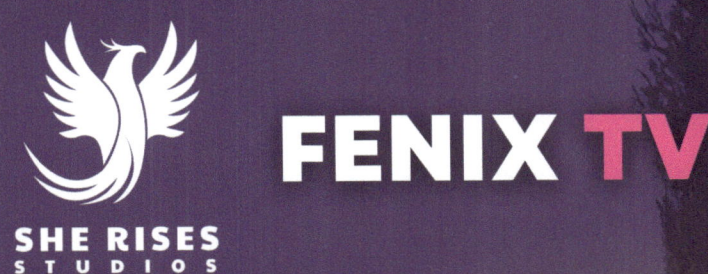

FENIX TV

SHE RISES STUDIOS

she wins

NICE GIRLS FINISH FIRST

SHE WINS
VIRTUAL SUMMIT 2025

When: May 14–16, 2025
Where: Exclusively on FENIX TV
Tickets: $49.97

Join us for the **She Wins Virtual Summit 2025**, a 3-day event celebrating women entrepreneurs and leaders from around the world. This year's theme, **"Nice Girls Finish First,"** showcases how kindness, empathy, and integrity drive success in business and life.

What to Expect:

- Inspiring stories from women leaders.
- Expert advice on leadership, resilience, and growth.
- Strategies for thriving in business without compromising values.

BE PART OF THIS EMPOWERING MOVEMENT AND DISCOVER HOW KINDNESS LEADS TO GREATNESS!

WWW.SHERISESSTUDIOS.COM/SHEWINSVIRTUALSUMMIT2025

CHERYL STRAYED:

Healing Through Story, One Letter at a Time

In the realm of emotional healing and radical honesty, Cheryl Strayed's voice has long been a beacon for those navigating the wilderness of grief, trauma, and self-discovery. As the bestselling author of Wild and the compassionate, unflinching voice behind the Dear Sugar podcast, Cheryl doesn't just tell stories—she helps people rewrite their own. Her work is a masterclass in resilience, shaped by lived experience and infused with deep empathy.

Dear Sugar, co-hosted with fellow author Steve Almond, began as a continuation of Cheryl's wildly popular advice column, but it quickly evolved into something more: a tender, soulful sanctuary for those aching for clarity, comfort, and connection.

Listeners write in with their deepest fears, regrets, and questions —about love, loss, addiction, betrayal, identity, and more—and Cheryl responds with the kind of wisdom that comes not from clinical textbooks but from lived, broken, and beautifully mended experience.

Cheryl's approach to emotional well-being is not to patch wounds with clichés, but to meet people where they are—with tenderness and truth. She acknowledges the mess, the uncertainty, and the pain of being human, and yet always manages to point toward light, meaning, and transformation. In her world, healing is not about erasing the past but about carrying it with grace and learning how to live forward with an open heart.

What makes Dear Sugar so profoundly impactful is Cheryl's uncanny ability to hold both the wound and the wonder at the same time. She doesn't flinch at the darkness—she walks right into it with you, lantern in hand. Her responses are literary, lyrical, and often deeply personal, drawn from her own losses and longings. She knows the terrain of grief because she's walked it. She understands shame and sorrow because she's lived them. And she offers guidance not from a pedestal, but from beside you, like a wise, soulful friend whispering, *"You are not alone."*

Mental Health Awareness Month is about breaking silence and creating space for real, unfiltered conversation—and Cheryl has been doing that for years. Her podcast is not just about giving advice; it's about bearing witness. It's about validating the human experience in all its complexity, and reminding us that our stories—no matter how painful—can be powerful tools for healing.

Cheryl often speaks of the transformative power of storytelling, and it's no surprise. Her own story, chronicled in *Wild*, resonated across the world for its raw vulnerability and fearless exploration of grief, self-reckoning, and resilience. Her journey—alone on the Pacific Crest Trail after losing her mother and unraveling from the inside out—became a metaphor for the journey so many of us take inside our minds and hearts when facing mental and emotional upheaval.

Through *Dear Sugar*, she continues that journey—not just for herself, but for her listeners. With every question she answers and every truth she tells, she chips away at the shame that keeps people silent. She reminds us that we don't need to have all the answers to begin healing. Sometimes, the first step is simply telling the truth—to ourselves, to others, to someone who will hold that truth with compassion.

Cheryl's work is deeply rooted in radical empathy. She sees the humanity in everyone, even in their most difficult moments. Her letters are infused with the belief that people are worthy of love, forgiveness, and redemption, no matter what they've been through. She doesn't rush healing, but she does nurture it, slowly and intentionally, through presence and prose.

In a time where mental health conversations are gaining much-needed momentum, voices like Cheryl Strayed's are essential. She reminds us that resilience is not about perfection or strength in the traditional sense. It's about showing up anyway. It's about walking through pain and continuing to choose love, meaning, and beauty—even when it hurts.

As we celebrate the voices of resilience this month, Cheryl's stands as a testament to the healing power of truth-telling. She doesn't offer easy fixes. What she offers is much more profound: the reminder that our stories matter, our pain is real, and our capacity to rise is infinite.

Through *Dear Sugar*, Cheryl Strayed holds a space where people can be seen, heard, and held—and that is one of the most powerful offerings anyone can give.

MEET ELISE MORGAN:

The Powerhouse Behind The Elise Morgan Experience Podcast

Elise Morgan is a former personal trainer, fitness model, professional athlete turned life coach, author, speaker, and healer on a mission to help you reclaim your power and create a life you love. Known for her bold, no-nonsense attitude and infectious energy, Elise brings personal development to life with a twist of sass, humor, and authenticity. Her podcast, The Elise Morgan Experience, is a journey of transformation where no topic is off the table, and every conversation leaves you empowered and ready to take action.

Elise's path to becoming the force she is today wasn't without its struggles. From overcoming toxic relationships and people-pleasing habits to navigating life's toughest challenges, Elise's story is one of resilience and self-discovery. Her own experiences have shaped her approach to coaching and personal development—showing that anyone, no matter what , can unlock their potential and live a life they love.

Elise dives into the real, raw aspects of life with a unique perspective. This podcast is for anyone looking to level up and break free from living a limited life. Whether you're dealing with divorce, grief, PTSD, the loss of loved ones, betrayal, or simply want advice and guidance on having confidence and showing up as the best version of yourself, Elise's podcast is a space to find inspiration, actionable advice, and powerful stories. She talks a lot about the law of attraction, manifesting, and mindset, all of which can help you create the life you deserve.

But Elise isn't alone in this journey. Some of her episodes features exciting guests who bring expertise from a wide range of areas, from personal development and dating to overcoming trauma and finding inner peace. It's a podcast that caters to but not limited to women ,for those ready to make a change and take control of their lives. Elise believes that the key to transformation is a shift in mindset, and she and her guests provide the insights and tools you need to make that shift.

"I believe in the power of the mind ," Elise says. *"Life doesn't have to keep you stuck. We all have the ability to design a life that aligns with who we really are, and that's what this podcast is all about— helping you wake up to the power within you!"*

With each episode, Elise challenges her listeners to take responsibility , bold action and stop waiting for permission to live the life they deserve. Whether it's learning how to set boundaries, heal from past wounds, or cultivate a positive mindset, Elise provides practical advice that's grounded in real-life experiences.

Elise's podcast is a blend of personal development, spirituality, and real talk. It's not just about listening; it's about implementing what you learn into your life , the shifts that will transform how you show up in the world. By weaving her expertise as a life coach with her candid, no-nonsense attitude, Elise helps you navigate the ups and downs of life with clarity, confidence, and grace.

As Elise continues to build her brand, she's creating a space for people to connect, learn, and grow. From one-on-one coaching to workshops and retreats, Elise's goal is to help people tap into their power and create their version of happiness, success, and fulfillment. It's all part of The Elise Morgan Experience, a movement as Elise describes *"to help you live a life you F-In love"*

So, if you're ready to transform your life, break free from self-doubt, and create the future you've always dreamed of, The Elise Morgan Experience is the podcast for you.

THE ELISE MORGAN EXPERIENCE

Connect With Elise

www.instagram.com/theelisemorganexperience
www.youtube.com/@TheEliseMorganExperience
www.podcasts.apple.com/us/podcast/the-elise-morgan-experience-real-talk-on-real-life/id1719459894
elisemorgan@coachelisemorgan.com

GET YOUR COPY NOW

Celebrate the power of women through inspiring stories and insights.

How I Unlearned My Crap
Kathy Baldwin

Stepping Up to Lead
Annabelle and India Beckwith

Redefined Flourishing In
Life While Becoming Wife
Breanna James

Redefining You
Amanda Cahill

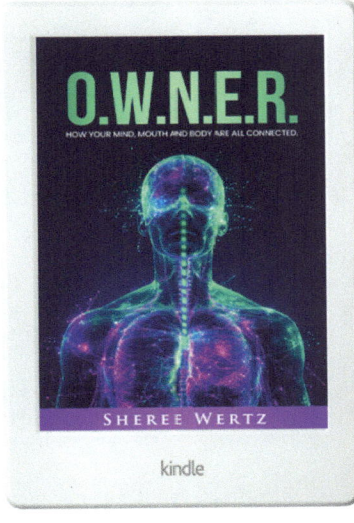

O.W.N.E.R.
Sheree Wertz

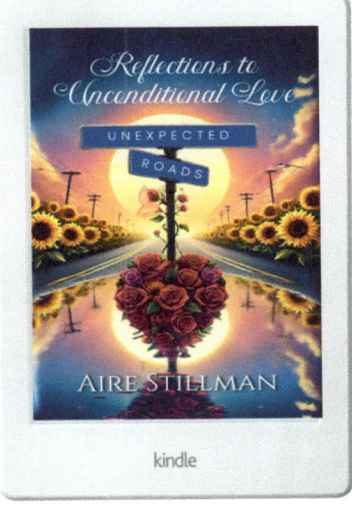

Reflections to Unconditional Love
Aire Stillman

UNSHAKEABLE:

The Story of a Woman Who Chose to Rise

By Monica Connolly

For many women, life becomes a balancing act of caregiving, career, and responsibilities, often at the expense of their own well-being and dreams. I know this struggle because I lived it.

For years, I was the one everyone relied on—the caregiver, the provider, the one holding everything together. I believed strength meant sacrificing my needs, pushing through exhaustion, and making sure everyone else was okay. It nearly cost me my life.

I'll never forget sitting in a doctor's office, exhausted and in pain, hearing the words that shook me to my core:
"If you don't make drastic changes, you are going to die soon."

At the time, I was battling severe obesity, chronic pain, and a heart condition. But what most people didn't know was that I was also struggling with a binge eating disorder. Food had become my comfort, my escape, and the way I coped with emotions I didn't know how to process.

I didn't even recognize the woman looking back at me. I wasn't just physically sick—I was emotionally and spiritually depleted. I had spent years pouring into everyone else, and there was nothing left for me.

That was my breaking point—but also my turning point.
I made a choice: I wasn't just going to survive—I was going to heal and thrive.

Over the next two years, I lost 150 pounds, but more importantly, I gained myself back. I healed my gut, rewired my mindset, and redefined who I was—not just for me, but for the women I knew were suffering in silence.

Through that transformation, I discovered a powerful truth: women are constantly told to put themselves last. They push through and try to be everything for everyone, and in the process, they lose themselves.

I knew I had to help change that narrative. That's why I became a Certified Holistic Health Coach, Master Life Coach, and Mindset Transformation Expert. My coaching isn't just about weight loss or wellness—it's about helping women reclaim their identity, reset their health, and realign with their purpose.

True transformation happens when we build lives that reflect our values and passions. For many women, that means stepping into entrepreneurship—not just to earn income, but to create businesses that leave a lasting legacy.

Through my Rise & Thrive coaching programs, I help women gain clarity, rebuild confidence, and take empowered action in their health, mindset, and leadership. Whether they're just starting their wellness journey or ready to launch a book, podcast, or business, I provide the accountability, tools, and strategy they need to grow.

That's why I also created:
- **Ember to Empire: A Women's Collective** – A networking and leadership community for ambitious women ready to rise.
- **The Rise & Thrive Mastermind** – A space for launching purpose-driven businesses and stepping into bold visibility.
- **The Unshakeable Belief Podcast** – Where I share real stories and strategies to help women build belief and take action.
- **My Upcoming Book, Made for More** – A guide to help women break free from limitations and embrace transformation.

If there's one thing I want every woman reading this to know, it's this:
You are not stuck. You are not broken. You are ready for more.

I know what it feels like to be exhausted and uncertain. But when a woman decides to take back her power, everything changes.

My mission is to educate, mentor, and empower the next generation of women leaders and changemakers. Because when women rise, families thrive, communities grow, and we build a ripple effect of impact that lasts for generations.

Now let's rise.

Connect With Monica

www.monicaconnollycoaching.com
www.facebook.com/monica.a.connolly.7
www.linkedin.com/in/mnconnolly
www.instagram.com/monicaconnollyandco

FINDING MY BEST SELF:

How Faith, Podcasting, and Purpose Fuel a Movement of Empowered Women

By Mandi St.Germaine

As co-host of the Finding My Best Self podcast and MBS | The Woman Beyond the Cape co-founder, I have witnessed firsthand the ways that podcasting extends far beyond content creation—it creates connection. To us, it's not just about releasing episodes; it's about creating a space that makes women actually feel seen, heard, and supported to just be themselves.

My place on this podcast grew out of my own experience. Decades as a military wife, mother of four daughters, educator, and business owner, I knew what it was like to be running on empty, invisible, and survival mode. But I also discovered how transformative it was when I chose to prioritize myself. That choice not only transformed my life—it became the catalyst for a movement. With MBS and through our podcast, we're giving women the strength to find their truth: when we love ourselves—body, mind, and spirit—we become bolder, more capable, and the best versions of ourselves.

Finding My Best Self creates weekly podcasts on personal growth, spirituality, emotional healing, and real stories of women who've struggled with courage and dignity. Our listeners tune in to everything from standing up to fear and healing from loss, to postpartum survival and regaining their identity after years of being *just mom.* These aren't light conversations—they're soul-deep. But we're mindful never to be overwhelming. We pray over each episode, research carefully, and consult with mental health experts so that everything we talk about does so with love and care. We're not therapists, but we present ourselves as a safe space—one that leads women one step closer to healing and wholeness.

One listener wrote to us, *"Your podcast pulled me out of a rut I didn't even know I was in. You gave me permission to slow down and breathe again."* That is why we do what we do. It's not perfection or polish—it's realness. Our show offers sacred space for women to breathe, to remember that self-care is not selfish—it's essential. And when women begin to show up for themselves in even the tiniest way, they begin to show up differently in every other aspect of their lives too.

Everything we do with MBS and our podcast is to help women live from the inside out. Our athleisure wear, which we have affirmations embedded in it and it's made to be multifaceted, reflects the message of the podcast: strength is in you already—you just need to believe it and wear it proudly. We've had women wear our leggings as a physical reminder of the emotional commitment they're making to themselves. And on the show, we bring that same passion to every single episode.

We're intentional about creating emotional safety, vulnerably leading, and giving encouragement that provokes real action. We always offer resources and disclaimers when addressing mental health topics, because our aim is to uplift without overwhelming. I also try to prioritize my own mental health care, because I know I cannot pour into others from an empty cup. That's the heart of MBS: empowering women to prioritize themselves without guilt or shame, and building community around that shared commitment.

As entrepreneurs, we've also utilized our platforms to make this community more robust—via Instagram, live events, and now podcasting. Finding My Best Self can be found on Apple, Spotify, YouTube, and Captivate. We invite women into the discussions that challenge, inspire, and empower them on a weekly basis. Whether they're washing clothes, commuting to work, or grabbing a couple of minutes of peace and quiet before the day becomes crazy, we hope that they'll finish each episode feeling less isolated and more revitalized.

Podcasting has given us a platform, yes—but more than that, it has given us purpose. And we will continue to show up with real talk and faith-filled encouragement and serve women in becoming their best selves, one episode at a time.

Connect With Mandi

www.mbsfit.co
www.instagram.com/mbs_my_best_self
https://podcasts.apple.com/us/podcast/finding-my-best-self/id1718755732

Women's Stories of Strength and Empowerment,
Accompanied by Actionable Strategies on How to Thrive

She GROWS STRONGER

HANNA OLIVAS
Along with 32 inspiring authors

GRAB YOUR COPY NOW

WWW.AMAZON.COM/DP/1960136666

In She Grows Stronger, Hanna Olivas and 31 inspiring authors share powerful stories of women who have transformed adversity into strength. Blending personal journeys with practical strategies, this book empowers readers to rise with confidence and resilience. A compelling guide for growth and self-discovery, it reminds every woman that no matter the challenge, she holds the power to grow stronger.

SHOP NOW

The SHE RISES STUDIOS PODCAST

TUNE IN. RISE UP. THRIVE.

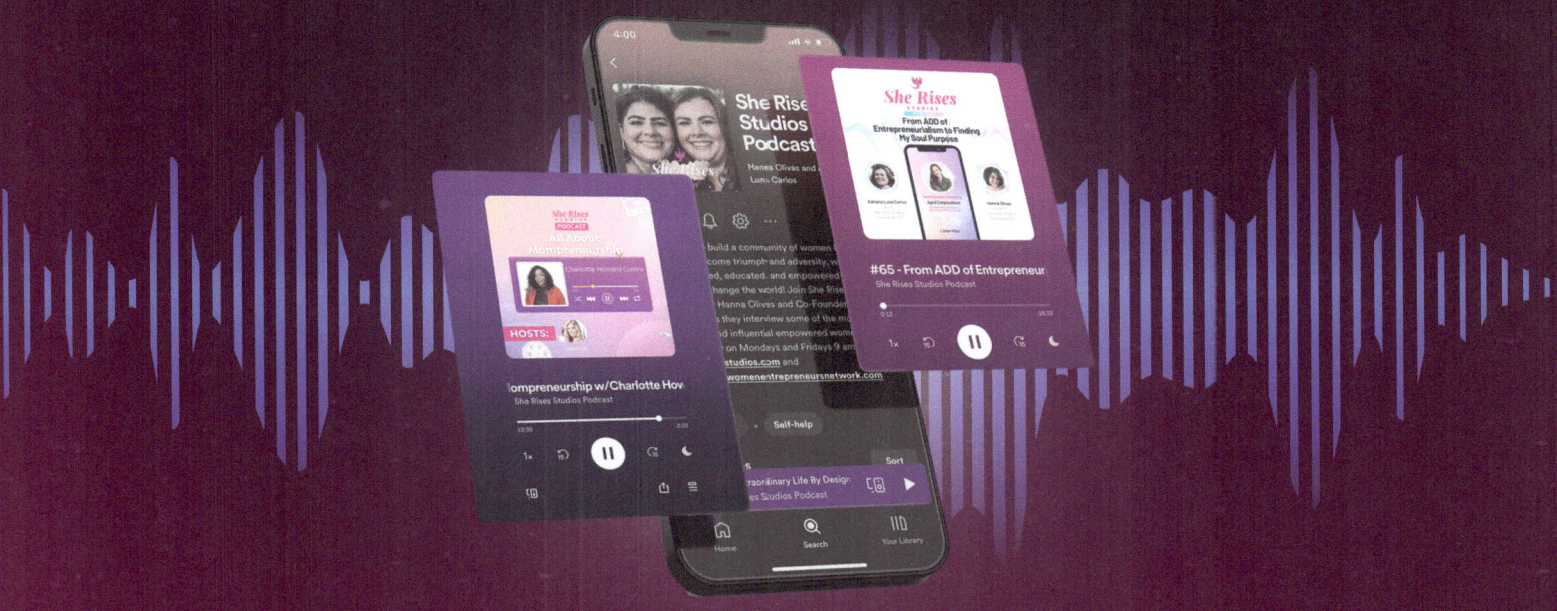

Looking for **real conversations** that inspire, empower, and ignite your potential? The **SRS Podcast** is where women like you come to **learn, grow, and rise!**

Join us for powerful **interviews with trailblazing entrepreneurs, thought leaders, and everyday women** who have turned obstacles into opportunities. Our episodes dive into:

➤ **Breaking through self-doubt** and stepping into confidence
➤ **Building a thriving business** with purpose and passion
➤ **Mastering work-life balance** without guilt
➤ **Leveling up your mindset, health, and career**
➤ **Finding your true purpose and living boldly**

Each episode is packed with **real stories, expert insights, and actionable strategies** to help you take your life to the next level. **This isn't just a podcast—it's your roadmap to success!**

SUBSCRIBE NOW AND START YOUR JOURNEY TO EMPOWERMENT!

BRENÉ BROWN:

Unlocking Us Through Vulnerability and Courage

In the realm of emotional resilience and mental wellness, few voices have echoed louder—or more powerfully—than that of Brené Brown. As a world-renowned researcher, bestselling author, and storyteller, Brené has spent more than two decades exploring the intersection of vulnerability, shame, courage, and connection. Through her groundbreaking podcast Unlocking Us, she continues to expand the conversation around mental health in ways that feel as profound as they are personal.

Brené Brown is more than a voice in the mental health field—she's a cultural force. Her research has transformed the way we think about what it means to live a wholehearted life. Her TED Talk, The Power of Vulnerability, remains one of the most viewed of all time, resonating with millions around the globe. And with her podcast, she brings that same depth and honesty directly to our ears, creating a space where truth-telling, laughter, and emotional growth live side by side.

What makes Unlocking Us so deeply compelling is not just the caliber of guests or the range of topics, but Brené herself. She brings her full self—unpolished, inquisitive, brave—to every episode. Whether she's interviewing a thought leader, reflecting on her own imperfections, or diving into the data behind emotional resilience, she reminds us that being human is messy, and that's exactly where the magic happens.

At the core of Brené's work is a message that we all need to hear, especially during Mental Health Awareness Month: Vulnerability is not weakness—it is the birthplace of strength. In a world that often demands perfection, productivity, and performance, Brené offers an alternative way of being. One where we can lay down our armor. One where we can tell the truth about our struggles without fear of being defined by them.

She teaches us that shame—the silent epidemic—thrives in secrecy. But when we bring our stories into the light, when we speak them out loud, they begin to lose their grip. Unlocking Us gives listeners permission to do just that. With every conversation, Brené shows that connection is not built through polished personas but through real, unfiltered humanity. And that is the foundation of emotional resilience.

Her episodes aren't just informative; they're deeply transformative.

Listeners are invited into a journey that doesn't just educate the mind—it touches the heart. From discussions on grief and burnout to joy, belonging, and self-compassion, Unlocking Us is a masterclass in what it means to live with intention, even when life is uncertain and overwhelming.

What's perhaps most remarkable is how Brené blends research with storytelling. She takes complex psychological concepts and wraps them in narratives that are relatable, raw, and real. She doesn't sit above her audience; she walks beside them. As someone who has openly shared her own struggles with anxiety and perfectionism, she leads not as someone who has it all figured out, but as someone who is figuring it out right alongside us.

This authenticity has made her podcast a lifeline for many. In a time where so many feel disconnected, isolated, or emotionally fatigued, *Unlocking Us* is a reminder that we are not alone. That our imperfections do not make us unworthy—they make us human. And that healing is not found in hiding, but in showing up fully, even when it's uncomfortable.

Mental Health Awareness Month is about bringing the invisible into the light. It's about starting conversations, breaking stigma, and finding the courage to take care of our inner worlds. Brené Brown is doing all of that and more. Through her voice, her research, and her fearless vulnerability, she is creating a culture where emotional wellness is not just talked about—it's practiced, celebrated, and valued.

As we honor the voices of resilience, Brené's stands tall. Not because it's the loudest, but because it's one of the most honest. She doesn't promise easy answers. What she offers is something far more powerful: the tools to sit with hard questions, the language to name our emotions, and the hope that we can all rise stronger.

Through *Unlocking Us*, she is not just unlocking ideas—she is unlocking hearts. And in doing so, she is changing the world, one story at a time.

MESSY MIDDLES AND BRAVE BEGINNINGS:

The Heart Behind Dionne Malush's Shine On Success Podcast

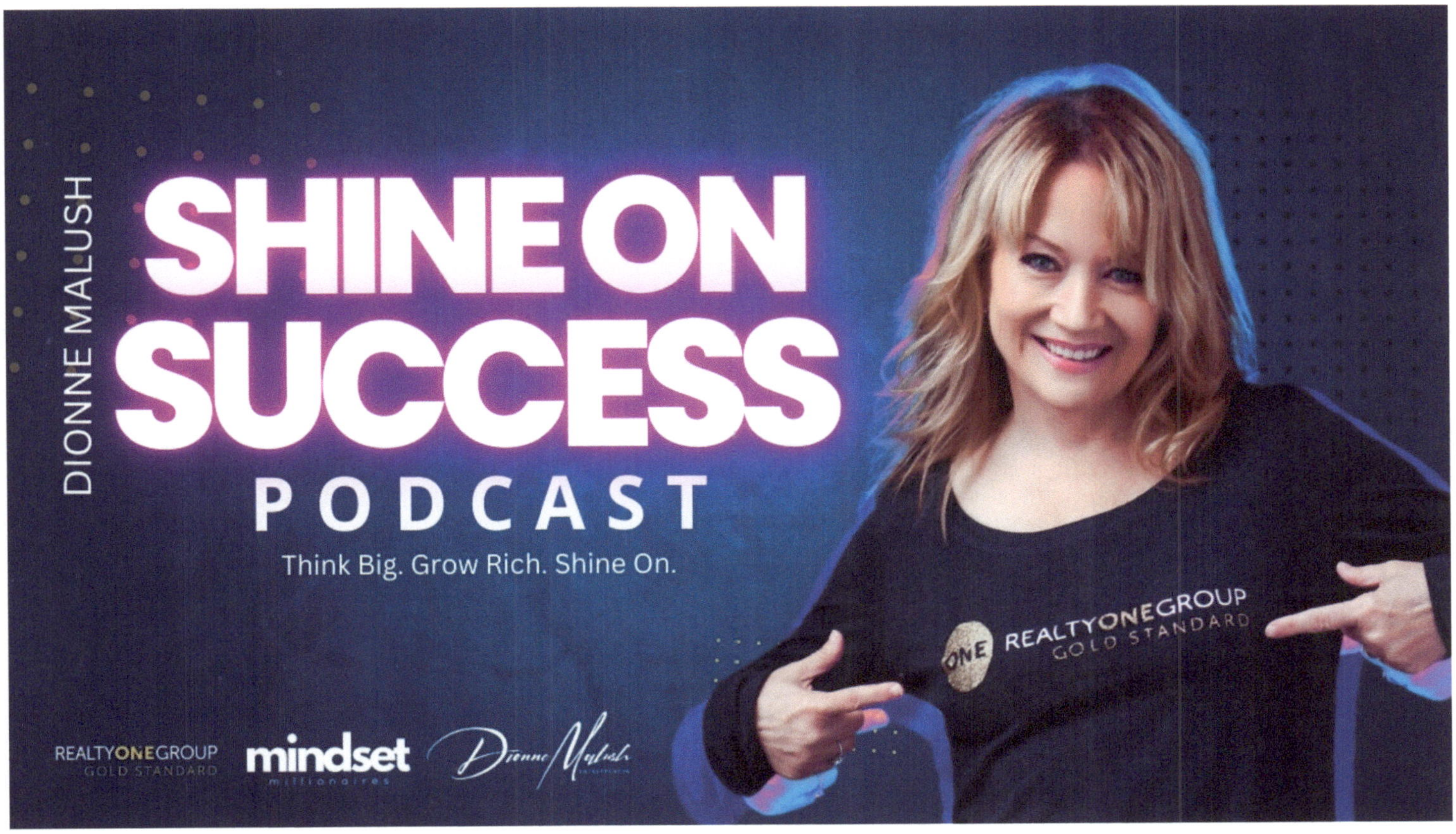

SHINE ON SUCCESS
PODCAST

Think Big. Grow Rich. Shine On.

REALTYONEGROUP GOLD STANDARD   mindset millionaires   Dionne Malush

SHINE ON SUCCESS

A PODCAST BY DIONNE MALUSH

In a world filled with highlight reels and filtered success stories, Dionne Malush stands out by choosing truth over polish, pain over pretense, and purpose over performance. As the host of the Shine on Success podcast, Dionne isn't just telling stories—she's holding space for the mess, the middle, and the magnificent breakthroughs that come after life nearly breaks you.

But before the microphone and the heartfelt interviews, there was loss. Deep, personal loss. When Dionne's father passed away, her world shifted. He had been her greatest cheerleader—the first person who ever truly believed she was destined for something big. His absence created a void that felt unbearable. Shortly after, her mother moved in, changing the dynamic of her daily life. And not long after that, her husband's health took a sudden turn. He needed a liver transplant. The hits kept coming.

Instead of letting the weight of it all drown her, Dionne chose creation as her lifeline. Shine on Success was born from that place—raw, honest, and full of heart. *"I needed something to hold onto,"* she shares. *"Something to build, to fill the void that grief left behind."* What she built became more than a podcast; it became a powerful, story-driven platform where bold entrepreneurs, resilient change-makers, and visionary leaders open up about the real journey behind their success.

Unlike many business-focused shows that skip straight to the how-to's and accolades, Dionne's podcast leans into the *"messy middle."* She's not interested in how many followers a guest has or how polished their LinkedIn profile is. *"If you've walked through something hard and found a way to turn that pain into purpose, I want your story on this show,"* she says.

That authenticity is the soul of Shine on Success. Dionne invites guests who've stared down storms that threatened to take everything. *"The common thread in their stories isn't perfection—it's resilience,"* she explains. *"They've been knocked down and still got back up, even when no one was watching. I relate to that more than anything."* As someone who's built businesses while grieving, caregiving, and reinventing herself, Dionne recognizes that kind of inner grit when she sees it—and she's made it her mission to spotlight it.

Each episode of Shine on Success is crafted with intention. Dionne's background in graphic design, branding, and AI informs not just the visual identity of the show, but also how she tells each story. *"I see this podcast as an extension of my brand, but also my heart,"* she says. *"Every episode is intentionally designed—visually and emotionally—to be powerful, professional, and deeply personal."*

That deep personal investment shows. Listeners walk away from episodes not only inspired, but equipped. The show seamlessly weaves heartfelt storytelling with real-world business strategy. Dionne's been in the trenches herself—burning out while trying to lead strong, mentoring agents only to feel the sting of betrayal, crying in her car after losses that felt like they should've mattered more to someone else. *"I know what it feels like to need both hope and a plan,"* she says. That balance of emotion and execution is exactly what keeps listeners coming back.

One episode that particularly impacted her was the conversation with Ken Kunken, titled *Why Not Me? Story of Grit, Grace, and Breaking Barriers.* Ken, who became paralyzed after a football injury but went on to become a prosecutor and advocate, reminded Dionne of what's possible when you refuse to be defined by tragedy. *"His story reinforced my belief that our struggles can become the foundation for our greatest strengths,"* she says. *"I have to admit there have been some tears throughout the process."*

Tears, yes—but also transformation. Hosting Shine on Success has not only given Dionne a new purpose, it's reshaped her as a leader. She's more grounded now, more intentional. *"I used to chase everything—and everyone—who wanted a spot on the show. Now I want to do what matters,"* she reflects. Each conversation reminds her she's not alone in that evolution.

As a certified Napoleon Hill coach, Dionne also integrates mindset mastery into every episode—whether her guests realize it or not. *"Most of my guests don't even realize they're living out Think and Grow Rich, but they are,"* she says with a smile. From definite purpose to persistence, from faith to autosuggestion, the core principles of success are embedded in the real-life stories she curates. Her job? To help listeners (and even her guests) connect the dots between mindset and momentum.

So, with countless podcasts flooding the space, what makes *Shine on Success* a standout? Dionne answers without hesitation: *"Because it's not about hype—it's about heart. I'm not chasing viral moments. I'm chasing truth."* And in an era where so many are tired of surface-level content, that truth is magnetic.

For those still in the *"messy middle"* of their own story, unsure of what success looks like or even if it's possible, Dionne has a message: *"Don't rush it. The middle is where your character gets built. I know it hurts. I've lived in that space where the fog is thick, the grief is heavy, and the future feels out of focus. But I promise—this part matters. Keep showing up. Keep planting seeds. Trust that even in the silence, something is growing. You're not behind—you're becoming."*

In every word she speaks and every story she shares, Dionne Malush proves that success isn't just about the wins—it's about who we become on the way there. And with *Shine on Success*, she's creating a space where that journey, in all its complexity and courage, can be celebrated out loud.

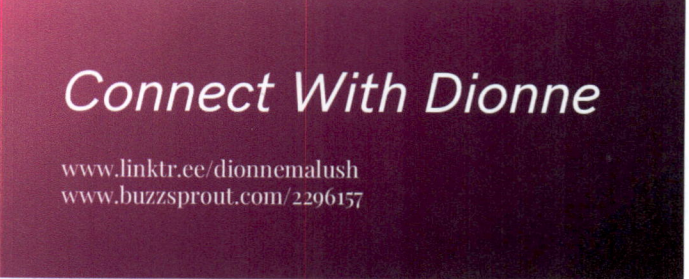

PODCASTARS

SHE RISES
STUDIOS

𝒰NLEASH YOUR STORY
BECOME A PUBLISHED AUTHOR!

Have you ever dreamed of sharing your wisdom, experience, or passion with the world? **Now is your time!**

Publishing a book isn't just about writing—it's about **establishing your authority, inspiring others, and creating a lasting legac**y. Plus, with the **$138.5 billion book industry** booming, there's never been a better moment to step into the spotlight.

At **SRS Publishing**, we don't just publish books—we **elevate voices, empower authors, and create change-makers**. Our mission is to help women break barriers, amplify their stories, and thrive in the publishing world. Whether you're an entrepreneur, thought leader, or storyteller at heart, **we're here to guide you every step of the way.**

JOIN THE FASTEST-GROWING PUBLISHING HOUSE FOR WOMEN IN THE USA.

READY TO TURN YOUR DREAM INTO REALITY?

---

 www.SheRisesStudios.com | *contact@sherisesstudios.com*

www.ingramcontent.com/pod-product-compliance
Lightning Source LLC
Chambersburg PA
CBHW041434120626
46547CB00002B/211